HOORAY FOR NUMBERS!

 Color the balloons with numbers **red**. Color the balloons without numbers **blue**.

Know Your Numbers **SESAME STREET**

1 | one

Trace the number **1**. Then write some of your own.

Count **1** doll. Then color the doll.

Explore More

Encourage your child to practice counting fun, healthy foods like raisins, carrots or dry cereal. Extend the learning by helping him or her place the items into groups, such as 2 apples, 5 carrots, etc.

 Circle the flowerpots that have **1** flower. Then color them.

 Look at the pictures. Circle the picture that shows **1**.

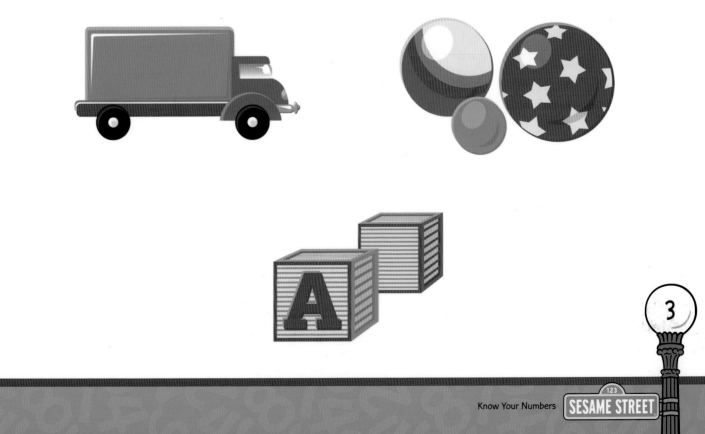

2 two

Trace the number **2**. Then write some of your own.

2 2

Count **2** tutus. Then color them.

4

Color the **2** eyes and **2** ears on each of the friends.

Draw **2** eyes and **2** ears to make a new friend.

Explore More ■ ◆ ● ◆ ■ ◆ ● ◆ ■ ◆ ●

Help your child count the things in one room of your home. Demonstrate by looking around the living room and counting: 1 sofa, 3 chairs, 2 tables, and 1 rug. Try counting things in other rooms too!

5

3

3 three

Trace the number **3**. Then write some of your own.

3 3

Count **3** tricycles. Then color them.

Circle the groups that show **3**.

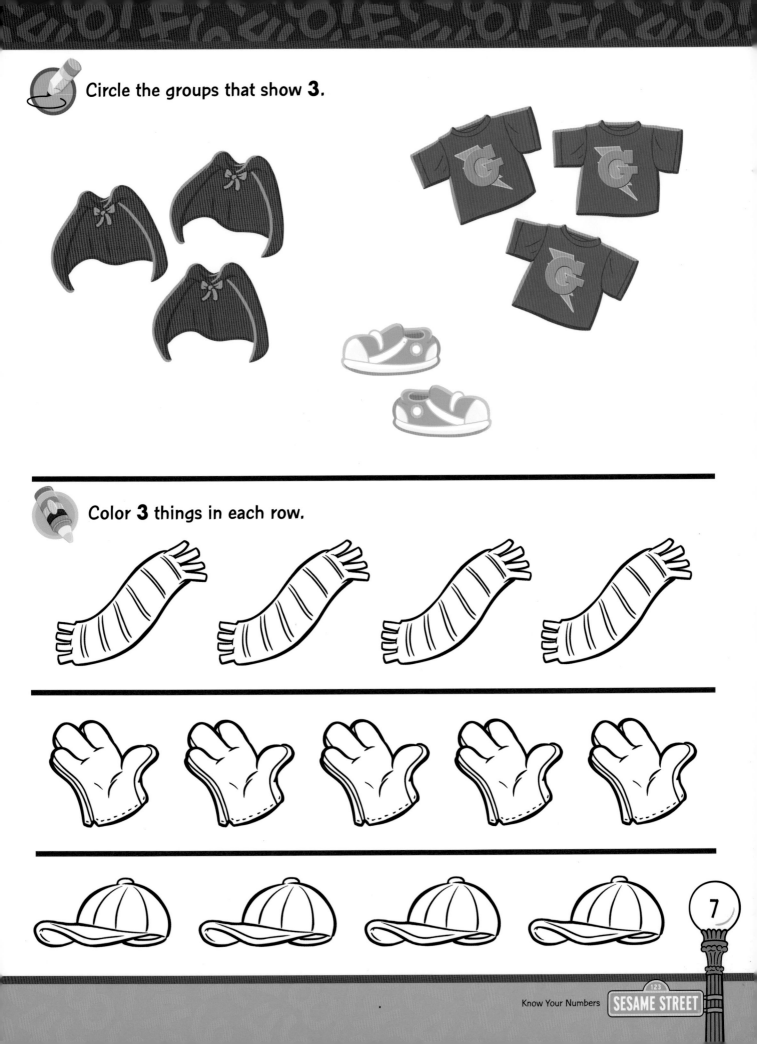

Color **3** things in each row.

7

4 four

Trace the number **4**. Then write some of your own.

4 4 4

Count **4** garbage cans. Then color them.

Trace 1 more barrel to make **4** altogether. Then color it.

Draw a line from each number to the group that shows how many.

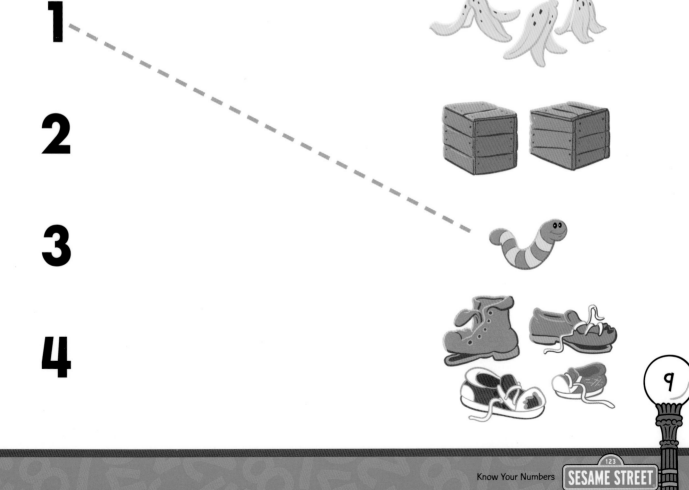

1

2

3

4

5 five

Trace the number **5**. Then write some of your own.

5 5

Count **5** flowers. Then color them.

Circle **5** dresses for Prairie Dawn to wear.

Circle the number to show how many in each row.

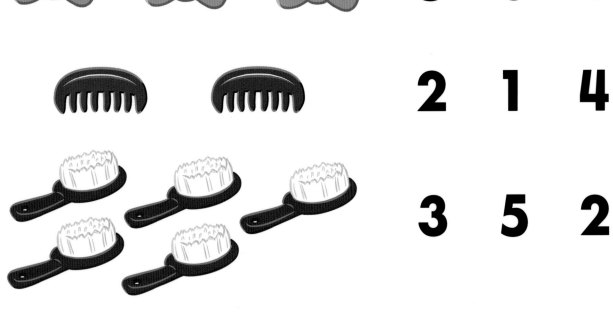

5   3   1

2   1   4

3   5   2

SESAME STREET

6 six

Trace the number **6**. Then write some of your own.

6 6

Cookie Monster likes lots of milk with his cookies!
Count **6** glasses of milk. Then color them.

Rosita loves to bake muffins.
Draw **6** chocolate chips on the muffin.

 Draw an **X** on **6** objects in each group.

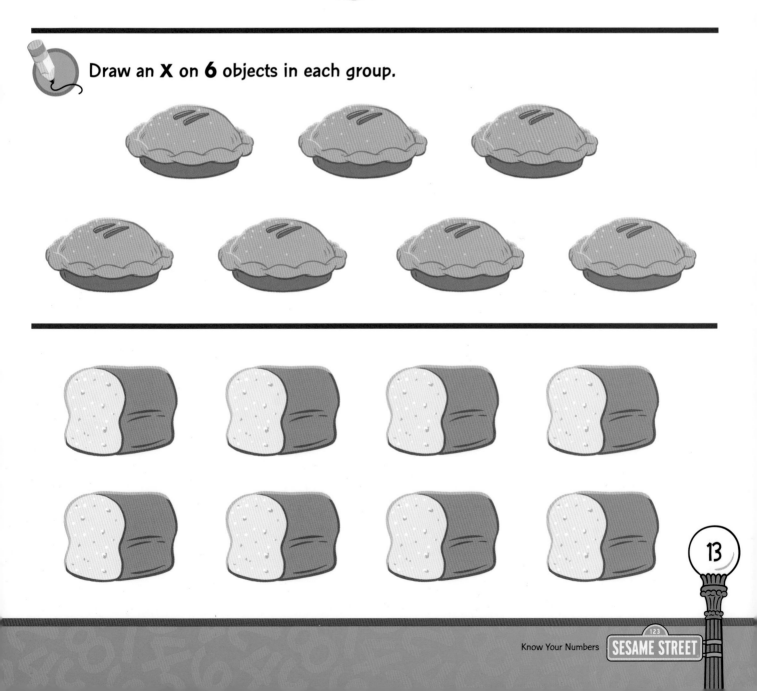

13

7 seven

Trace the number **7**. Then write some of your own.

Count **7** nests. Then color them.

Count and color **7** bats.

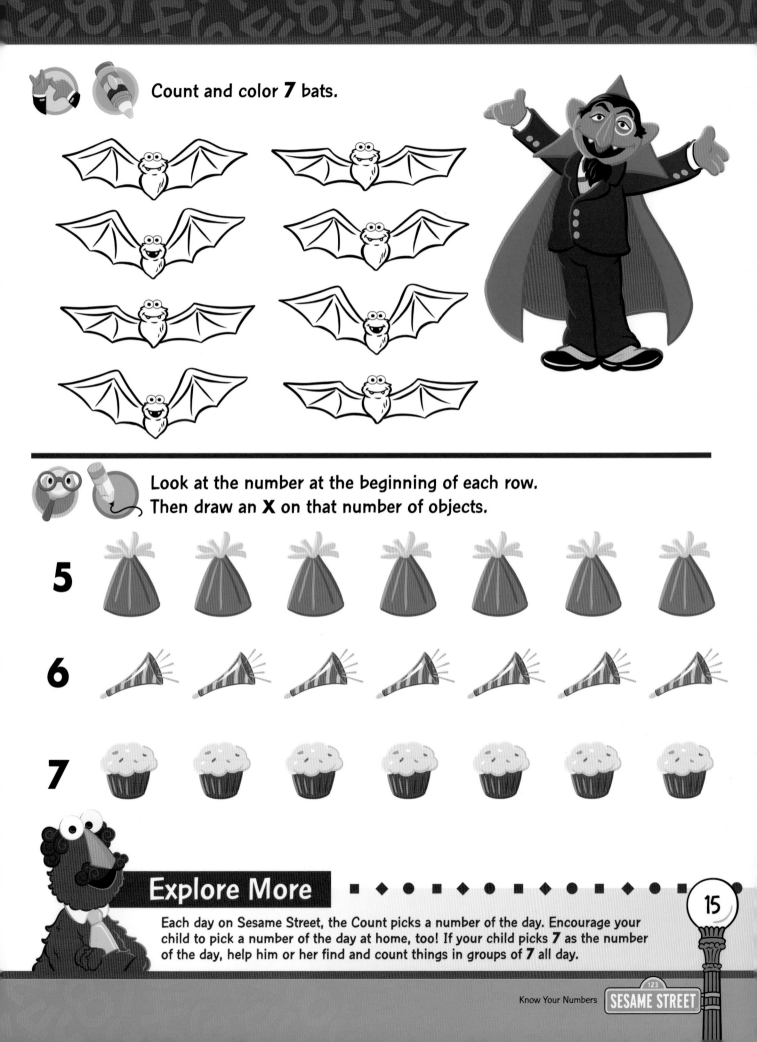

Look at the number at the beginning of each row.
Then draw an **X** on that number of objects.

5

6

7

Explore More

Each day on Sesame Street, the Count picks a number of the day. Encourage your child to pick a number of the day at home, too! If your child picks **7** as the number of the day, help him or her find and count things in groups of **7** all day.

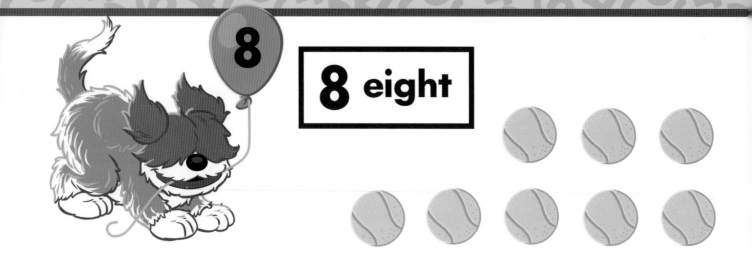

8 eight

Trace the number **8**. Then write some of your own.

8 8

Count **8** dog bones. Then color them.

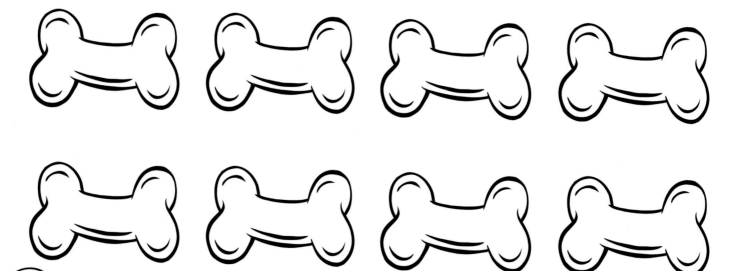

Trace the door on **8** of the doghouses.

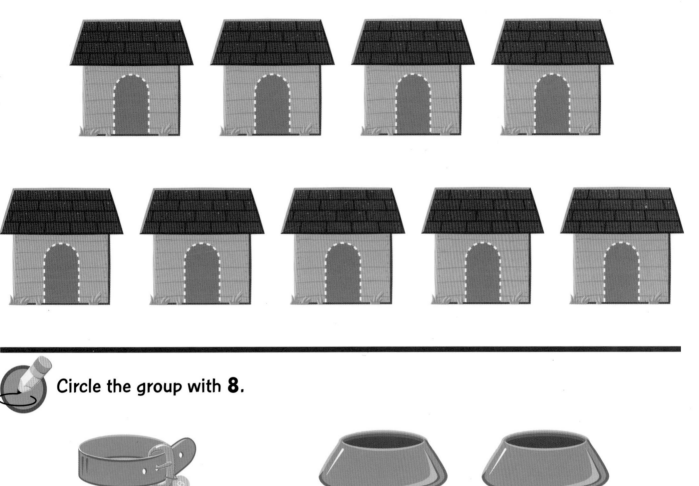

Circle the group with **8**.

17

9 nine

Trace the number **9**. Then write some of your own.

Count **9** dishes. Then color them.

Explore More

Ask your child to help you set the table. Count the dishes as you put them on the table and encourage your child to count with you. Do the same with the silverware, glasses, and cups.

Draw more teacups to make **9** altogether.

Circle the group with **9**.

19

10 ten

Trace the number **10.** Then write some of your own.

10 10

Count **10** skateboards. Then color them.

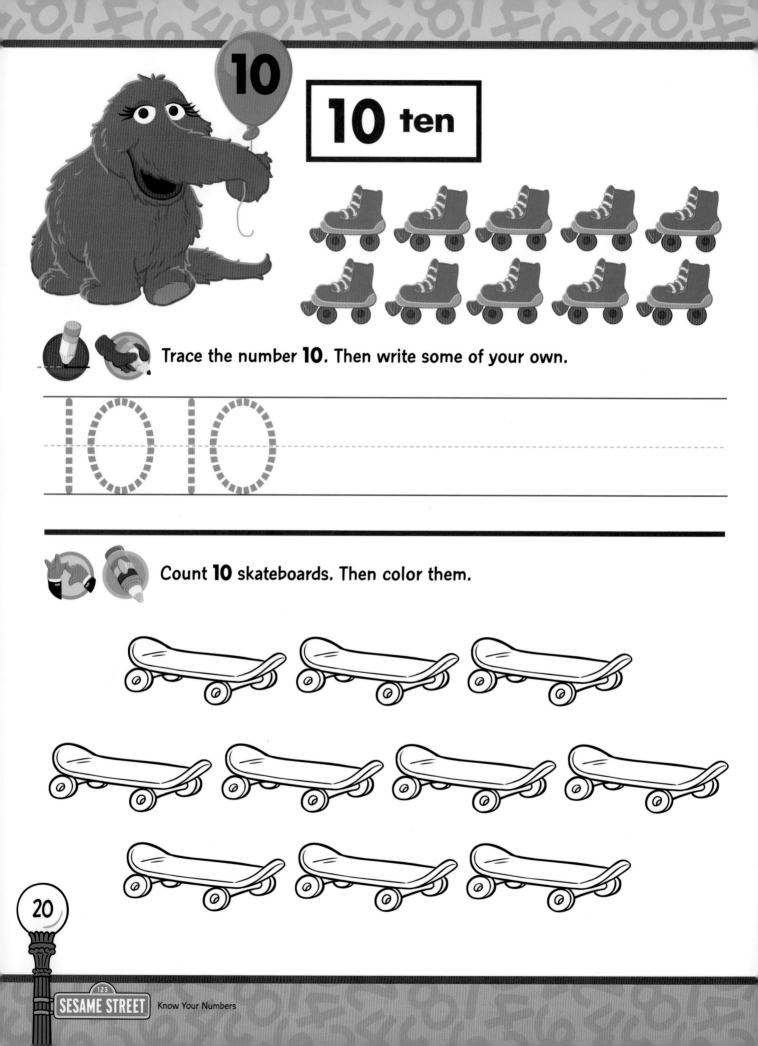

Draw more bubbles to make 10 altogether.

 Draw an X on 10 things in each group.

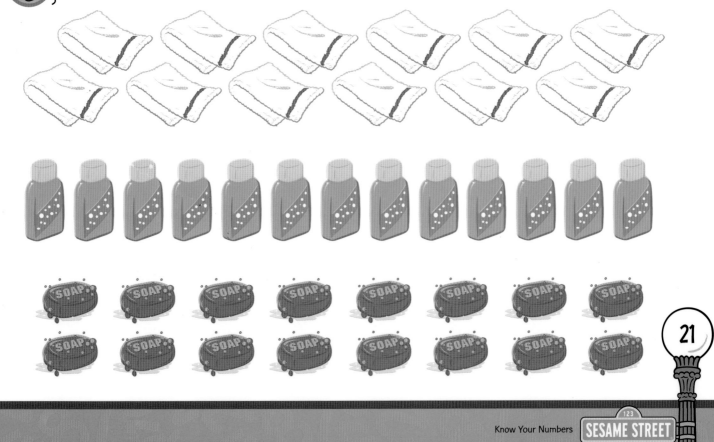

How many do you see?

Count each fruit. Then write how many.

_____

_____

_____

_____

How many do you see?

 Count each animal. Then write how many.

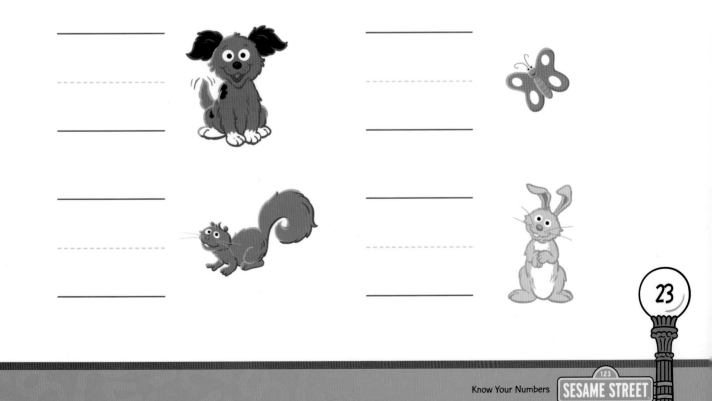

Draw a line to connect the **orange** dots from **1** to **10**.
Draw a line to connect the **green** dots from **1** to **10**.
Then color the picture.

Explore More

Go on a number hunt with your child. Look for things in your home like telephones, books, and computers that have the numbers **1–10** on them. Encourage your child to point to and say each number.